DJANGO

BONNIE CHRISTENSEN

Rb.
Flash
Point

A NEAL PORTER BOOK   ROARING BROOK PRESS   NEW YORK

Belgium
January 23, 1910

Dogs bark
Banjos talk
Dinners boil in black pots.
A laugh, a screech, a baby cries,
Django is born.
His father's violin sings.
Bells ring in a far off town.

Always moving place to place,
Country to country.
No school, no reading, no writing.
Hard life everywhere.
Work at this. Work at that.
Hard life.

Wood smoke always in his eyes, his clothes.
Wisps of smoke escape their fires,
Float on music to the stars.
Ahhhhh music . . .

Music . . .
      sighing
      weeping singing
      laughing breathing
      reeling spinning.

Heels kicking, toes clicking
Feels like home.
Dancers twirling,
Faster faster
Dizzying darkness past the fires.
Heartbeats drumming, breathless singing,
Float on music to the stars.

Little Django, trout tickler, hedgehog hunter,
Catches fish or meat for dinner.
Games of chance and movie lover
Left abandoned by his father.

Now in Paris making music,
Sweet duets on busy corners.
Listening here, learning there,
Picking melodies fine and full,
Dreams evolving into songs.

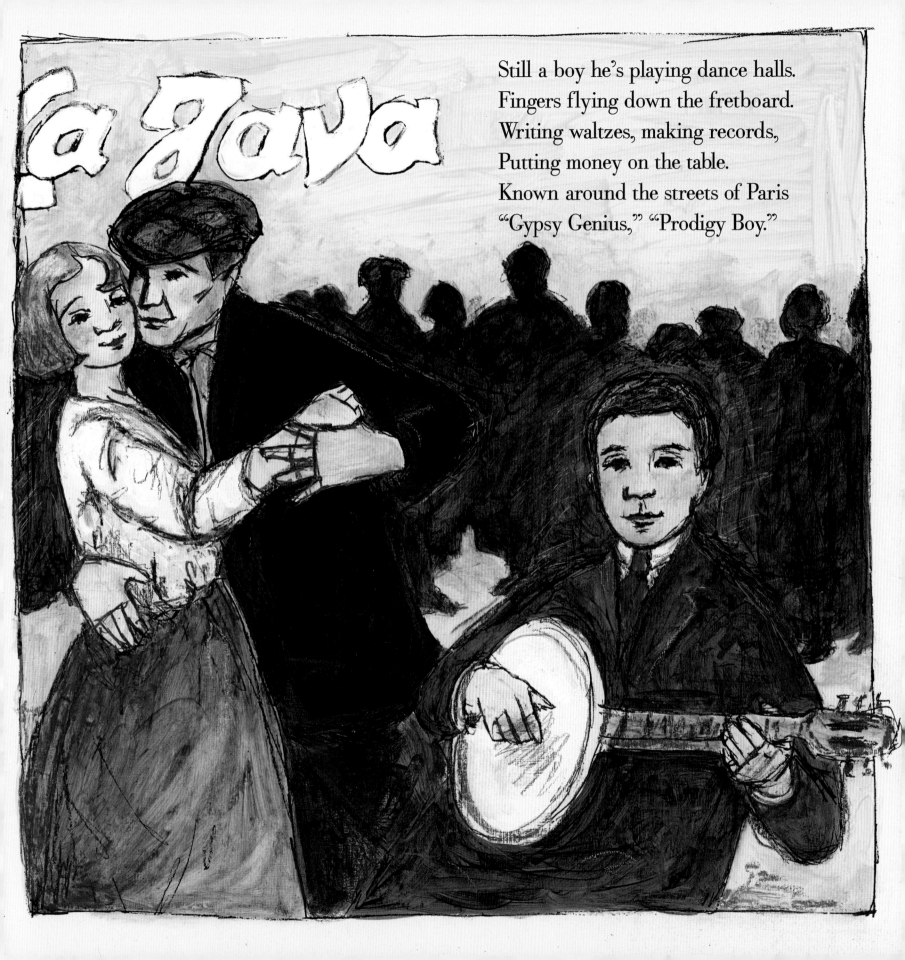

Still a boy he's playing dance halls.
Fingers flying down the fretboard.
Writing waltzes, making records,
Putting money on the table.
Known around the streets of Paris
"Gypsy Genius," "Prodigy Boy."

Django doesn't hear the chatter
Listening to the saxes sigh.
Trombones moan, clarinets wail
Jazz riffs curling through the night.

Jazz Americain, jazz like Django—
    moving bending
     changing blending
Try that rhythm, stretch that measure,
syncopation. Twist that line.

Paris, 1928

Through the smoky sweaty dance hall
Cuts the king of Europe's jazz bands.
Straight to Django, makes an offer
"Join my band, and make the big time."
Django smiles.

Lost in dreams,
In worlds of wonder,
Django leaves the lights of Paris,
Taxis to the dark encampment.
Darker still inside his wagon,
Only light a bit of candle.
Django dreaming of tomorrow
As the candle falls.

Within a heartbeat something flashes
One flame leaps, and then a thousand.
Smoke and fire rip the night sky.
Blazing burning everywhere.

A scream, a screech, then footsteps running
Django struggles toward the doorway—
Falls then rises up again.
Pulled at last from the inferno
He's become a flame himself.

Doctors shake their heads and murmur,
"Such awful burns, that leg, that hand."
The hand he used to fret guitar—
Burned so deeply, nearly useless.
Doctors shake their heads and frown.

Dreary ward in dreary hospital,
Endless hopeless months crawl by.
Mending, healing doing nothing—
Silence. Useless. What tomorrow?

Then his brother brings a present,
Lays it silent on the bed.
The doctors shake their heads and murmur,
"He'll never play guitar again."

Endless silent months creep by.
Django staring at the wall.
Useless.

One day, at last with bandage gone,
All alone, no one listening,
Django takes guitar in hand.
Right hand slowly strumming slowly,
Stiffly picking cross the strings.
While the famous left hand hardly moves,
Two fingers lay as still as stone.

Every day he works that left hand,
Works the first two awkward fingers,
Works for weeks to get them moving,
Works for months to make them fly.
Gradually he finds a new way,
Playing scales, and chords, and tunes.
He finds a sound unique and new.
Keeps it to himself.

Paris, 1930

Back at home the music's soaring
Singing, dancing, celebrating.
Django breaks away a moment
Then he's back with his guitar.

Music slows, "What's he doing?"
Looks of pity cross the circle.
"Left hand's useless. What's he thinking?"
Some shake their heads, some look away.

Then Django starts in, slowly slowly.
Smiles flash across frowning faces.
Two fingers race along the fretboard,
Twist the tune and send it flying
Through the night sky to the stars.
Relief, amazement, in the shadows,
Gleeful claps that urge him on.

Django's only just beginning,
Bright and brilliant stages waiting
Django's gypsy jazz guitar.
To float on music to the stars,
Float on music to the stars.

AND THEN . . .

After Django figured out how to play guitar again, nothing could stop him. First he played with an orchestra in the South of France, then in Paris where many famous singers and artists came to see him. He also made numerous recordings.

But 1934 changed everything. In that year Django met jazz violinist Stephane Grappelli, and the two started playing music together whenever they could. Eventually both became members of the "Quintette du Hot Club de France," along with Django's brother, Nin Nin. When the quintet's first record was released, Django became a true musical star, playing with the best of American jazz musicians, touring throughout Europe, and broadcasting to the United States.

The group was in England when World War II began. Despite the danger, Django returned to Paris, where he played music throughout the war. In 1946, Django toured the United States as a special guest soloist with Duke Ellington and his orchestra, ending the tour at Carnegie Hall in New York City.

Back in France, Django continued to play and record. For many years, he worked hard touring, playing big cities,

recording and writing. Then in 1951, he moved with his wife and young son to a small town outside Paris where he could fish and paint and play guitar at cafés in the evening. A few years later, he was invited to play in a worldwide tour, but it wasn't to be. Django died on May 16, 1953, leaving a musical legacy, which is today carried on by his grandson David, as well as many, many other fine musicians.

NOTES ON THE ROMA

The ethnic group of people known as "gypsies," or Roma, originally migrated from India about a thousand years ago. Their migration first took them to Persia, then, over time, to Africa, Europe, and eventually the Americas.

Today, approximately 15 million Roma, of many different tribes, live around the world. They have their own language and traditions. Family plays a very important role in their culture; as does music.

Roma are known as travelers, but their traveling was not by choice. Very often they were persecuted and driven from town to town. They lived first in tents and later in wagons drawn by horses. In some countries, they were enslaved. It is estimated that the Nazis killed nearly one and a half million Roma during World War II.

The majority of Roma now live in permanent homes. They have a Romani flag and national anthem and are represented by various organizations. The International Romani Union works directly with the United Nations Economic and Social Council.

MORE NOTES . . .

Name
The name "Django" is a gypsy name which means "I awake." Django's official, legal name was Jean Reinhardt.

Banjo/guitar
Django's first instrument was the violin, but when he was twelve he was given a "banjo-guitar." This instrument had the body of a banjo but the neck (which includes the fretboard) and six strings of a guitar. It was also played like a guitar.

Fish or trout tickling
If Django didn't have a fishing pole, he would wait patiently by a stream, running his hand underwater along the bottom until he felt a fish. Then slowly he would tickle the fish's belly to calm it until he could quickly grab it out of the water.

78 rpm records
The records Django recorded were 78 rpm phonograph records. These black records were made of a brittle substance which broke easily, but both sides of the record could be played.

BIBLIOGRAPHY

Delaunay, Charles. *Django Reinhardt*. Cambridge, Mass: De Capo Press, 1982.

Dregni, Michael. *Django, the Life and Music of a Gypsy Legend*. New York: Oxford University Press, 2004.

Dregni, Michael. *Gypsy Jazz: In Search of Django Reinhardt*. New York: Oxford University Press, 2008.

SELECTED DISCOGRAPHY

A complete discography of Django Reinhardt includes over 200 albums. Listed here are five albums that reflect the span of his career.

Djangology (Remaster)
July 9, 2002, Bluebird RCA

The Best of Django Reinhardt
March 19, 1996, Blue Note Records

Verve Jazz Masters 38
November 9, 1994, Verve

Django Reinhardt and Stephane Grappelli
January 21, 1992, GNP/Crescendo

Rare Django
June 29, 1990, DRG

For Robert Resnik

Special thanks to Andrea for Paris, Lance for sharing studio space,
Will Mentor and St. Michael's College for ongoing support.
Also many, many thanks to Marcia, Neal, and Jennifer!

A Neal Porter Book
Published by Flash Point, an imprint of Roaring Brook Press
Roaring Brook Press is a division of Holtzbrinck Publishing Holdings Limited Partnership
175 Fifth Avenue, New York, New York 10010
www.roaringbrookpress.com

Distributed in Canada by H. B. Fenn and Company, Ltd.

Cataloging-in-Publication Data is on file at the Library of Congress.
ISBN-13: 978-1-59643-422-6

Roaring Brook Press books are available for special promotions and premiums.
For details contact: Director of Special Markets, Holtzbrinck Publishers.

Printed in February 2010 in the United States of America by Phoenix Color Corp. d/b/a Lehigh Phoenix, Rockaway, New Jersey.
Book design by Jennifer Browne
First edition September 2009
2   4   6   8   10   9   7   5   3

Linda was the first to find one of Big Joe's buoys. Erik remembered that the colors they were looking for were green, white, and red.

In the fourth lobster trap, they finally caught two lobsters. One lobster was much too small, but the other one looked big enough to keep.

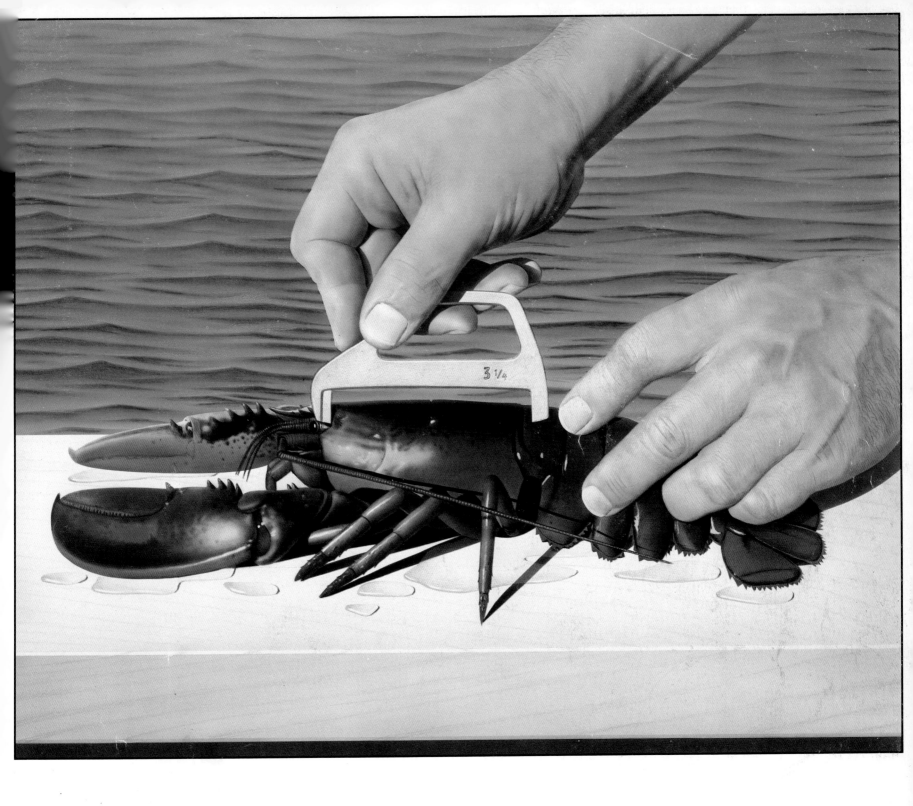

Big Joe showed them the special gauge that a lobsterman uses to measure a lobster. A lobster is measured from its eye socket to the end of its back. The other lobster was also too small.

Before throwing the lobster back in, Big Joe showed Linda and Erik how to hold a lobster. The easiest way to pick it up is by its body with one hand. Then the lobster cannot bite you with its claw or hit you with its flapping tail.

Big Joe helped Erik put rubber bands on the claws so that the lobsters could not bite anyone. Lobsters have two claws. One is a "cruncher claw" that is strong and dull. The other claw is a "scissors claw." It is sharp and quick.

Lobsters also have two antennas. They have eight legs. The first two legs on each side have little pinchers on them. They have tails that flap. One amazing thing about lobsters — when they lose an antenna, leg or claw, a new one grows back.

In the eighth lobster trap, they caught twenty-two crabs, six small lobsters, and four lobsters that were large enough to keep. Claws were snapping everywhere, and Big Joe had trouble pulling everything out without getting bit.

Erik wanted to know if lobsters eat hamburgers, fries, and pizza. Big Joe and Linda laughed. Big Joe told them to remember that lobsters eat anything. They would even eat pizza if they could find some.

Soon they were at the entrance of the harbor. Linda told Big Joe that going lobstering was really fun. Erik agreed.

They were back on the pier. Big Joe was happy because he had caught the biggest lobster he had ever seen. Linda was happy. Erik was happy. Now all of their friends want to go lobstering.